BEYOND BUSINESS

10 VENTURES THAT INSPIRED ME

YOHAN VED

Made with ♥ on the Notion Press Platform
www.notionpress.com

To my Mother and Grandfather, who always believed in working for a cause.

Contents

Prologue *vii*

1. OUR FUTURE IN THE STARS 1

2. BUSINESS WITH PURPOSE 5

3. MORE THAN JUST A PAIR OF GLASSES 7

4. ONE FOR ONE 10

5. ONE SCOOP AT A TIME 13

6. A FUTURE WE CAN TASTE 16

7. THE HEARTBEAT OF THE HANDMADE 18

8. THE LIVING SOUNDTRACK 20

9. THE HAPPY SHOE 22

10. REVOLUTION IN EVERY AISLE 24

THE LEGACY OF INNOVATION 27

Prologue

For as long as I can remember, I have been fascinated by the way businesses function. Not just in terms of making money or selling products, but in the way they influence people, industries, and even the world. Some companies are not just businesses. They are movements. They are pioneers of change. This book is about ten such businesses that have left a lasting impression on me, not just because of what they sell but because of what they stand for. When most people think of businesses, they often imagine corporate giants focused on numbers, sales and expansion.While success in those areas is important, I have always been more inclined towards companies that go beyond just making money. I am interested in businesses that have a deeper purpose, companies that are built on strong values, and brands that strive to make a change. These are the kinds of businesses that inspire me. They do not just sell a product. They tell a story. They change the way we live, work, and think.

One of the businesses that immediately caught my attention was TOMS. The idea that buying a simple pair of shoes results in another pair being donated to someone in need fascinated me. It made me realize that business does not have to be purely about financial gain. It can be built on the idea of giving back. Beyond the world of fashion and retail, there are businesses that have completely transformed entire industries. SpaceX has changed the way humanity looks at space travel, making it more affordable and realistic for the future. Spotify has redefined the way people listen to music, moving us away from CDs and downloads to a world of endless streaming. Beyond Meat has proven that plant-based food can be a real alternative to traditional meat, making sustainability a central part of its mission. These businesses did not just follow trends. They created them. They challenged the impossible and introduced new ways of thinking.

This book is my attempt to understand and appreciate the businesses that have shaped the world in ways I admire. I want to understand what makes them unique, how they started, and what guidance they offer to anyone who believes that business should be about more than just money. Whether it is through sustainability, innovation, customer experience, or social impact, these companies have shown that business can be used for greater things than profit. As I write about these ten businesses, I hope to share not just facts and achievements, but also my personal admiration for what they represent. Each of these companies has, in some way, changed the way I think about business and the role it plays in our lives. They have shown me that success is not just measured in rupees and sales, but also in the way a company positively or negatively affects people.

This book is not just about business. It is about vision, courage, and the willingness to do something different. It is about companies that took risks, challenged expectations, and ultimately made an impact that extends far beyond their products. These are the businesses that inspire me, and I hope that by the end of this book, they will inspire you too.

CHAPTER ONE

OUR FUTURE IN THE STARS

Ever since I was a child, I have been captivated by the stars. The idea that the universe is vast, that beyond our planet there are billions of other worlds filled with mysteries and endless possibilities, has always inspired a sense of awe within me. As a kid, I would sit on my terrace, staring at the night sky, imagining the stories of distant stars, planets, and galaxies. I wondered about the endless horizon of space and what it would be like to venture into the unknown. The thought of space travel, the concept of reaching other planets, was a dream I could not shake. I didn't just want to study space from a distance, I wanted to be a part of it.

My fascination with space wasn't just about the stars or the planets. It was about the adventure, the human drive to go beyond what we know and venture into the vast unknown. I vividly remember watching rockets launch on TV or reading about astronauts venturing into space. The courage, the determination, and the curiosity that defined these explorers resonated deeply within me. I would often dream of being one of those astronauts, gazing out from the window of a spacecraft, witnessing Earth from above, knowing that I was part of something bigger than myself. The idea that one day, humanity would travel beyond the confines of Earth, and perhaps even set foot on another planet, was something that I held onto with all my heart.

Space has always been a place of wonder, mystery, and possibility. Yet, for the longest time, it felt like an unreachable dream. I grew up hearing about space programs from the 1960s, the Apollo missions, and the idea that humans had once walked on the Moon. But despite all of this, space travel seemed so distant, something for future generations to experience. I never imagined that in my lifetime, the dream of traveling beyond Earth might become a reality. But then something incredible happened. I learned about SpaceX.

SpaceX wasn't just another company in the aerospace industry. It was a beacon of hope for everyone who had ever dreamed of space. Founded by Elon Musk in 2002, SpaceX set out to do what had previously been thought impossible: reduce the cost of space travel and ultimately make it possible for humans to live on Mars. When I first heard about this mission, something deep inside me stirred. SpaceX's vision wasn't just about reaching for the stars, it was about expanding the human experience beyond the confines of Earth. It was the realization of a dream that I had held onto since childhood.

SpaceX's approach to space exploration was different. It wasn't content with simply achieving small milestones, it sought to revolutionize the entire process of space travel. The company's first major breakthrough came with the development of reusable rocket technology. Before SpaceX, rockets were single-use, discarded after each launch. The thought of launching something that could be used only once seemed wasteful, not to mention astronomically expensive. But SpaceX flipped that paradigm on its head. With the Falcon 9 rocket, they proved that rockets could be reused, launched, landed, and flown again. This was nothing short of a miracle for the space industry, and for me, it felt like a personal triumph. The idea that we could reduce the cost of space travel and make it more sustainable was a breakthrough that gave hope to dreamers like me. It meant that space was no longer an unattainable goal, it was something we could realistically aim for.

But SpaceX wasn't satisfied with just creating reusable rockets. They had a much bigger vision in mind. Their goal wasn't merely to improve the current state of space exploration, they wanted to change the very foundation of space travel. The company's long-term mission to establish a human colony on Mars is something that resonates with me on a personal level. For as long as I can remember, I have been fascinated by the idea of humanity becoming a multi-planetary species. The prospect of humans living on Mars and beyond, of creating new homes in the stars, is something that seems both wildly ambitious and deeply necessary. The reality of living on Mars, of human life extending beyond Earth, isn't just an abstract idea anymore. With SpaceX's vision for Starship, their next-generation spacecraft designed to carry humans to Mars, that dream feels within reach.

In 2012, SpaceX achieved a milestone that forever changed my view of the space industry. Their Dragon capsule became the first privately developed spacecraft to deliver cargo to the International Space Station. This was groundbreaking, not just because it marked the first time a private company had done something that had previously been the sole domain of government agencies, but because it demonstrated that the private sector could play a pivotal role in the future of space exploration. Watching that achievement unfold was a defining moment for me. It made me believe, once again, that humanity's future lies in the stars.

As SpaceX continued to push the boundaries of space technology, I found myself following each new achievement with excitement. In 2020, SpaceX launched the first crewed mission from U.S. soil since the Space Shuttle program ended. The Crew Dragon capsule carried two NASA astronauts to the International Space Station, and it was a historic moment for both the United States and private spaceflight. As I watched that launch, I could feel my heart racing. For a moment, it felt like the entire world was holding its breath, watching the future of space travel unfold before our eyes. It was a moment of triumph, not just for SpaceX, but for all of humanity. It was a reminder that space is no longer the stuff of dreams, but a reality that we are actively working toward.

SpaceX's achievements don't end with the launch of cargo or astronauts. The company is actively working to develop Starship, a massive spacecraft that will be capable of carrying large numbers of people to Mars and beyond. The very idea of humanity traveling to another planet, establishing a colony on Mars, is the stuff of science fiction, but with SpaceX, it feels like we're inching closer to that dream. To me, this isn't just about building rockets. It's about fulfilling a larger, more profound mission. It's about the survival of humanity and our desire to explore the unknown. The drive to make life interplanetary isn't just a scientific ambition, it's a moral one. If we want to ensure the future of our species, we must reach beyond the confines of Earth and make our mark on the cosmos.

SpaceX has also helped to democratize space exploration in ways we could have only imagined a decade ago. With the launch of the Starlink satellite constellation, SpaceX is working to bring global broadband internet coverage to even the most remote corners of the world. For me, this is just another example of how SpaceX is not just advancing space travel but also using its innovations to improve life on Earth. The idea that a single company can simultaneously push the boundaries of space exploration and improve the lives of people here on Earth is both inspiring and humbling.

The emotional connection I feel to SpaceX is profound. Growing up, I could never have imagined that I would witness such groundbreaking advancements in space exploration in my lifetime. When I was a child, space felt like a far-off dream, something that belonged to future generations. But with SpaceX, I feel like I'm living in that future now. Their vision, their drive, and their successes are not just changing the course of space travel, they are changing the way I see the world. Every achievement, every milestone, brings me closer to my own childhood dream of reaching the stars. SpaceX has shown me that space is no longer a distant frontier. It is our future.

In conclusion, SpaceX represents more than just a company to me. It embodies the dream of every child who has ever looked up at the stars and wondered what lies beyond. It represents the ambition to not only explore space but to build a future there. For me, SpaceX is a symbol of possibility, of what can be achieved when imagination meets innovation, and of what humanity is capable of when we dare to dream big. Through SpaceX, I've come to realize that space is not an unreachable frontier. It's a place we're heading to, together, as a species. And I can't wait to see where the journey takes us.

CHAPTER TWO

BUSINESS WITH PURPOSE

Patagonia is not just a clothing company, it is a belief system, a way of doing business that challenges everything we think we know about capitalism. When Yvon Chouinard founded the company in 1973, he wasn't trying to build a global brand. He was a climber who wanted to make better gear for himself and his friends. But as Patagonia grew, so did its mission. Today, it stands as a powerful example of what happens when a business puts the planet first.

From the very beginning, Patagonia refused to follow the traditional rules. They didn't just want to make high quality outdoor gear, they wanted to make it responsibly. Long before sustainability became a buzzword, they were experimenting with recycled materials and finding ways to reduce waste. They understood that every product had an environmental cost, so they asked their customers to think before they bought. They even set up repair centers around the world, teaching people how to extend the life of their gear instead of replacing it. This wasn't just good for the planet it built a sense of loyalty among customers who saw Patagonia as more than just another brand.

In 2011, they made a move that shocked the retail industry. They ran an ad that said, "Don't Buy This Jacket." It wasn't a joke or a reverse psychology marketing stunt. It was a direct call for people to rethink their shopping habits. Patagonia was asking its own customers to buy less, to be mindful of the environmental impact of their choices. It was a radical, almost rebellious act in an industry built on endless consumption. But that's Patagonia, never afraid to challenge the status quo.

Patagonia's commitment to the planet isn't just talk. Every year, they donate 1% of their sales to environmental causes, a commitment that has led to over $100 million in contributions. But in 2022, Yvon Chouinard took things even further. He gave the entire company away. Instead of selling Patagonia or passing it down to his children, he placed it in a trust that ensures all future profits around $100 million a year go toward fighting climate change. It was an unprecedented move, proving that Patagonia's values are more than just a marketing strategy. They are the company's foundation.

Ethical production is another area where Patagonia refuses to compromise. They ensure their workers are paid fairly and treated with respect, partnering with Fair Trade Certified factories and continuously assessing their supply chain for improvements. They've also committed to making their entire business carbon neutral by 2025. From using renewable energy in their facilities to sourcing materials more responsibly, every decision is made with the planet in mind.

And when they see something that threatens the environment, they take action. In 2017, when the U.S. government reduced protections for national monuments, Patagonia didn't just release a statement they sued the government. It was a defining moment in corporate activism, proving that companies have both the power and the responsibility to stand up for what's right.

Patagonia has completely changed the way people think about business. They've shown that a company can be wildly successful without sacrificing its principles. They've inspired other brands to take sustainability seriously and have set a new standard for what ethical business should look like. At a time when consumers are more conscious than ever about the impact of their purchases, Patagonia has become the gold standard for purpose driven business.

But beyond the policies and activism, Patagonia is about something deeper. It's about a way of living, choosing adventure, protecting the planet, and doing what's right, even when it's hard. They aren't just making gear. They are building a movement. And in doing so, they've proven that business can be more than just profit, it can be a force for good.

CHAPTER THREE

MORE THAN JUST A PAIR OF GLASSES

Warby Parker is one of those rare companies that make you stop and think about why things have always been a certain way. Before they came along, buying glasses felt like a frustrating, overpriced chore. You would walk into a store, try on a few pairs under fluorescent lighting, and end up paying way too much for something that felt more like a necessity than a personal choice. But Warby Parker changed all of that. They made glasses something people could get excited about, something stylish, something affordable, and most importantly, something that could do good in the world.

It all started with four friends Neil Blumenthal, Dave Gilboa, Andy Hunt, and Jeff Raider who realized that glasses didn't have to cost a fortune. They had all experienced the same problem: losing or breaking a pair of glasses and then dreading the cost of replacing them. When they looked into why eyewear was so expensive, they found that a few massive corporations controlled the entire industry, keeping prices artificially high. That did not sit right with them. So they decided to take matters into their own hands.

The idea was simple but revolutionary. Warby Parker would cut out the middlemen and sell directly to customers, bringing down prices without sacrificing quality. Suddenly, instead of paying hundreds of dollars for a pair of glasses, people could buy stylish, well-made frames for less than 100 dollars. This was a game-changer. They launched with a small collection, but their business model flipped the industry upside down. Customers were not just buying glasses; they were buying into a movement that challenged the norm.

But Warby Parker did not stop at just making glasses affordable. They wanted their company to stand for something bigger. That is where their

Buy a Pair, Give a Pair program came in. For every pair of glasses sold, they would donate another to someone in need. They understood that something as simple as a pair of glasses could change a person's life, helping children see the blackboard in school or allowing adults to work more efficiently. Rather than just handing out glasses, they worked with nonprofit partners to train people in underserved communities to give eye exams and distribute affordable eyewear. This approach ensured lasting impact, rather than just a one-time handout.

And then came another big problem: shopping for glasses was a hassle. Warby Parker tackled this issue head-on with an idea so simple, it was surprising no one had done it before. They introduced the Home Try-On program, where customers could pick five frames online, have them shipped to their homes for free, try them on at their convenience, and then send them back. No pushy salespeople, no pressure, just an easy way to find the perfect pair. It was one of those ideas that, once it existed, made people wonder how they had ever lived without it.

Beyond their smart business model and their commitment to social good, Warby Parker had something else that set them apart: personality. They made glasses fun. Instead of feeling like a medical necessity, their frames became a fashion statement, a form of self-expression. They leaned into a cool, bookish aesthetic, using witty marketing, creative store designs, and a friendly, down-to-earth approach. Their retail stores feel more like boutique bookstores than traditional eyewear shops, inviting customers to browse and enjoy the experience rather than just pick up a product and leave.

As they grew, Warby Parker expanded beyond glasses, introducing sunglasses and even their own line of contact lenses. But no matter how much they scaled, they never lost sight of their mission. They kept pushing for sustainability, looking for ways to make their supply chain more ethical and environmentally friendly. They focused on making their materials more responsibly sourced and committed to reducing their carbon footprint.

Their success also changed how brands connect with their customers. Unlike traditional eyewear brands that relied on celebrity endorsements and expensive advertising, Warby Parker built its reputation through word of mouth and social media. They understood that customers wanted to feel a connection to the brands they supported. Their marketing is filled with humor, creativity, and storytelling, making people feel like they are a part of a community rather than just buyers of a product.

Perhaps the most remarkable thing about Warby Parker is that they took on an industry that had remained unchanged for decades and proved that things could be different. They did not just disrupt the eyewear market; they redefined what it means to be a socially conscious business. They showed that companies can make money and make a difference at the same time. In doing so, they set a new standard for how modern businesses should operate, proving that customers are willing to support brands that align with their values.

Looking ahead, Warby Parker continues to innovate. They are investing in virtual try-on technology, expanding their selection, and finding new ways to make an impact. But at their core, they remain the same company they set out to be, a brand that believes glasses should not be overpriced, that shopping for them should be enjoyable, and that businesses have a responsibility to do good in the world.

Warby Parker is more than just an eyewear company. It is a movement. It is proof that businesses do not have to choose between profit and purpose. And it is a reminder that sometimes, the best ideas come from simply asking, "Why has it always been this way?" and daring to do things differently.

CHAPTER FOUR

ONE FOR ONE

Blake Mycoskie did not set out to start a movement. He was just traveling through Argentina in 2006, soaking in the culture, when he noticed something that would change the course of his life forever. He saw children walking around barefoot, their feet rough and exposed, vulnerable to cuts and infections. It was heartbreaking. It was also something he could not ignore. He kept thinking about those kids, about how something as simple as shoes could make a world of difference. And that is when the idea hit him. He was not going to just donate a few pairs, he was going to build an entire business around giving back.

Instead of starting a charity, Blake believed in creating something sustainable, something that would keep making an impact without relying on donations. That is how TOMS was born. The idea was beautifully simple. For every pair of shoes sold, another pair would be given to a child in need. This was not just a business plan, it was a purpose. It was a way to bridge the gap between consumerism and kindness, to make giving back as natural as buying something for yourself.

The first TOMS shoes were inspired by the alpargatas he had seen in Argentina, lightweight, comfortable slip-ons that felt effortless but stylish. At first, it was just Blake, a few friends, and a dream. They worked out of his tiny apartment, hustling to get the word out. He would carry boxes of shoes to meetings, hoping someone would see the vision. And they did. The response was overwhelming. People were not just buying the shoes, they were buying into something bigger. They wanted to be a part of this mission. Celebrities started wearing them, magazines wrote about them, and suddenly, TOMS became more than a brand, it became a movement.

As the company grew, so did its impact. TOMS worked with organizations around the world to ensure that their shoe donations went to the right places. But Blake quickly realized something. Just giving away shoes was not enough. It had to be done the right way. They partnered with experts, nonprofits, and local leaders to make sure the donations fit the specific needs of each community. It was never about a one time handout, it was about creating real, lasting change.

And then came the next step. Blake and his team knew the One for One model could do more. So they expanded. TOMS introduced an eyewear line, where every purchase helped provide eye care, glasses, medical treatment, even surgeries, for people who needed them. Later, they moved into coffee, using each sale to fund clean water initiatives in developing regions. What started as a shoe company had turned into something so much more, a blueprint for how businesses could give back in meaningful ways.

But success did not mean the journey was always smooth. As TOMS grew, so did the scrutiny. Some critics questioned whether giving away shoes was really the best way to help communities. Others worried that the model was too simple, that it was not tackling the root causes of poverty. Blake listened. He took the feedback seriously. And rather than getting defensive, TOMS adapted. They started funding long term initiatives, supporting local businesses, and investing in sustainable solutions. The mission was never just about giving things away, it was about making a lasting impact.

Through it all, one thing never changed. TOMS remained rooted in the belief that business should be about more than just making money. People wanted to support companies that stood for something, that made them feel like their purchases mattered. TOMS showed the world that something as small as buying a pair of shoes could set off a ripple effect, changing lives across the globe.

Today, TOMS is still evolving, still learning, still pushing forward. They have shifted their focus to funding grassroots organizations and sustainable development programs, making sure their impact goes even deeper. They have also embraced sustainability, ensuring their products are ethically made and environmentally friendly.

At its core, TOMS is about more than shoes, or glasses, or coffee. It is about challenging the way business is done, about proving that companies can be profitable and purposeful at the same time. It is about reminding us all that the simplest ideas, like giving a child a pair of shoes, can turn into something that changes the world. And it all started because one man paid attention, saw a problem, and decided to do something about it. That is the real legacy of TOMS.

CHAPTER FIVE

ONE SCOOP AT A TIME

I cannot remember the first time I had Ben and Jerry's, but I do remember the feeling. It was not just ice cream. It was an experience. The ridiculous chunks of cookie dough, the creamy swirls of chocolate fudge, the names that made me smile before I even took a bite. It felt different from every other brand out there, and as I learned more about the company behind the pint, I realized why. Ben and Jerry's is not just about making ice cream. It is about making a statement. It is about proving that a company can be fun, delicious, and unapologetically dedicated to making the world a better place.

Ben Cohen and Jerry Greenfield were just two childhood friends who decided to take a five dollar ice cream making course because they wanted to do something they loved. No business degrees, no grand plan, just a passion for creating something good. And that is exactly what they did. They opened their first scoop shop in a renovated gas station in Burlington, Vermont, and from the very beginning, they infused their brand with personality and heart. This was not corporate, this was personal. It was real.

What made me fall in love with Ben and Jerry's was not just the ice cream, though that would have been enough. It was the way they ran their business. They were not just selling pints, they were standing up for what they believed in. Long before corporate social responsibility became a trend, Ben and Jerry's was leading the charge. They used ethically sourced ingredients, partnered with family farms, and made sure their employees were treated well. It was about making sure that every scoop had a positive impact beyond just satisfying a sweet tooth.

And they never stayed silent when it mattered most. While most companies tried to avoid controversy, Ben and Jerry's embraced activism like no other. They spoke out against climate change, championed LGBTQ+ rights, and tackled racial injustice head on. They did not just write vague corporate statements, they backed up their words with action. They created flavors that raised awareness for important causes, like "Save Our Swirled" to highlight the urgency of climate change and "Justice Remix'd" to support criminal justice reform. They never shied away from taking a stand, and that made me respect them even more. I loved knowing that every pint I bought was contributing to something bigger than just my dessert cravings. It felt good to support a company that actually cared.

Of course, not everyone was a fan of their outspoken approach. Some people said a company should stick to making ice cream and stay out of politics. But that is the thing about Ben and Jerry's. They never saw social justice as politics, they saw it as humanity. They believed that business had the power to create real change, and they refused to let profits come before people. That is a kind of integrity that is rare, and it is why I will always be loyal to this brand.

When I heard they sold the company to Unilever, I was worried. I thought maybe this would be the end of the Ben and Jerry's I loved. I imagined the flavors becoming less bold, the mission getting watered down, the soul of the brand fading into just another corporate label. But they proved me wrong. They did not just sell and walk away, they fought to make sure their social mission stayed intact. Even under corporate ownership, they refused to compromise on what made them special. They are still pushing boundaries, still challenging the status quo, still proving that a company can do good without losing its heart. That means something to me. It makes me feel like supporting them is not just about indulging in a sweet treat but about standing by a company that has never backed down from its beliefs.

Ben Cohen and Jerry Greenfield did not just build an ice cream empire. They built something bigger, something that has inspired me and so many others. They showed the world that business does not have to be cold and impersonal, that it can be filled with heart, laughter, and purpose. And most importantly, they reminded me that even the smallest choices, like which pint of ice cream I grab from the freezer, can be a way to support something I believe in. That is the magic of Ben and Jerry's. It is more than just ice cream. It is a reflection of everything I value, boldness, kindness, and the courage to stand up for what is right. And that is why I will always be a fan.

CHAPTER SIX

A FUTURE WE CAN TASTE

I have always believed that food is more than just fuel. It is culture, it is comfort, it is tradition. But what if the food we love could be better for the planet, for animals, and for our own health? That is exactly what Beyond Meat set out to prove, and honestly, I think they have done something incredible.

I have followed Beyond Meat's rise with fascination. The idea of plant-based meat that looks, cooks, and tastes like real meat is something that once felt impossible. But Ethan Brown, the founder of Beyond Meat, did not see it that way. He saw the massive environmental impact of traditional meat production, from deforestation to excessive water use to greenhouse gas emissions, and he knew there had to be a better way. Instead of trying to convince people to stop eating meat, he set out to recreate it from plants, using science to mimic the taste, texture, and even the way meat cooks on a grill. The result? A burger that sizzles, browns, and satisfies like beef, but without the downsides.

What makes Beyond Meat so special to me is not just the product itself, but the mission behind it. This is not just about selling plant-based burgers. It is about making real change in the food industry. Meat consumption is deeply ingrained in our culture, and for many people, giving it up entirely is not an option. Beyond Meat does not ask people to sacrifice, it simply gives them a better alternative. One that is better for the environment, better for their health, and better for animal welfare.

And people are noticing. Beyond Meat has landed in grocery stores, fast food chains, and restaurants all over the world. It is not just for vegetarians and vegans, it is for anyone who wants to make a small change that adds up to a big difference. The fact that I can walk into a restaurant and see a Beyond Burger on the menu next to traditional beef burgers feels like proof that we are moving in the right direction.

Beyond Meat is not stopping at burgers. They have expanded into sausages, meatballs, chicken, and even steak. Every new product they release brings us one step closer to a world where plant-based meat is not the exception, but the norm. If they can create a future where we can enjoy all the flavors we love while protecting the planet, then that is a revolution worth supporting.

What inspires me the most is that Beyond Meat is not just focused on today. They are thinking long-term. They invest in research, working with scientists to improve their products and get even closer to the real thing. They are not satisfied with being good enough. They want to be better, always. That kind of relentless innovation is something I admire. It is not just about business growth, it is about a bigger vision for the world.

Beyond Meat is also breaking through barriers in industries that were once completely dominated by animal products. They have partnered with major fast food chains, proving that plant-based options are not just a niche trend, but something mainstream consumers are embracing. Seeing them take on the giants of the meat industry and hold their own is nothing short of inspiring. It is a reminder that change is possible, even in the most unlikely places.

But at the heart of it all, Beyond Meat represents a choice. A choice to eat differently, to think differently, to question the way things have always been done. It is not about forcing anyone to give up meat. It is about showing people that there is another way, a way that does not compromise on taste or experience but does so much good in return.

Beyond Meat is not just a food company to me. It is a movement. It represents innovation, sustainability, and the belief that we can do better without giving up the things we enjoy. Every time I see someone choosing Beyond Meat, I feel like we are all part of something bigger. I am supporting a company that is proving we do not have to destroy the planet to enjoy good food. And that is a future I want to be a part of.

CHAPTER SEVEN

THE HEARTBEAT OF THE HANDMADE

The world moves fast. Mass production floods shelves, and soulless factories churn out identical products without a story. But somewhere in this whirlwind of consumerism, there is Etsy, a quiet, resilient sanctuary where craftsmanship and creativity still matter. Etsy is not just a marketplace, it is a revolution against disposability, a stand for uniqueness, and a testament to the power of small businesses and individual artisans. It whispers to the dreamers, the crafters, and the ones who believe that something made by human hands carries more meaning than something stamped out by a machine.

Etsy's story is deeply intertwined with the people it empowers, an artist selling handmade jewelry in a small town, a woodworker creating custom furniture in his garage, a mother finding financial independence through her sewing skills. Every product carries a human touch, a passion, a late night spent perfecting a design. This is not just commerce, it is connection. The stories of the creators matter as much as the items themselves. When you buy on Etsy, you are not just purchasing an object, you are buying a piece of someone's heart, their perseverance, and their belief that art and individuality still have a place in this world.

Etsy's impact goes beyond transactions. It creates communities. It brings together people who value the extraordinary in a world that often prioritizes efficiency over soul. The platform thrives because it understands that customers don't just want products, they want stories, they want authenticity, they want to feel something. In a society that so often diminishes the value of handmade work, Etsy fights back by celebrating it.

It is a reminder that creativity should be nurtured, not sacrificed. It is proof that success can be built not on mass production, but on passion, skill, and a deep commitment to preserving the art of making. And in a time when automation and artificial intelligence threaten to strip the human element from everything, Etsy stands firm, reminding us that there is still immense value in the handmade, the heartfelt, and the beautifully imperfect.

CHAPTER EIGHT

THE LIVING SOUNDTRACK

usic is not just sound. It is memory, emotion, escape. It is the background to our happiest moments and the solace in our darkest hours. And in a world that has made music more accessible than ever, Spotify has become more than a streaming service, it has become a lifeline, a storyteller, and the thread that connects people across time and space.

Imagine the weight of a difficult day lifting as your favorite song plays. Think of a late night drive, city lights flickering past as a melody carries you somewhere beyond the present. Picture the feeling of discovering a song that seems to understand you better than words ever could. That is the magic of Spotify, it is not just a company, it is an architect of experience, a curator of emotion, a bridge between artist and listener.

Before Spotify, the music industry was a tangled web of gatekeepers. Albums had to be bought, tracks had to be hunted down, and discovery was limited by what the industry deemed worthy of promotion. But Spotify shattered those barriers. It made music democratic. It gave independent artists the same platform as global superstars. It didn't just hand power back to musicians, it handed it to the people, allowing anyone with an internet connection to find and fall in love with songs from every corner of the world.

But more than that, Spotify became deeply personal. Playlists became love letters, road trip companions, and time capsules of moments both fleeting and profound. The algorithms learned our moods, our favorites, our heartbreaks, and our joys. In a world where everything feels increasingly disconnected, Spotify quietly did something remarkable, it understood us.

It is easy to dismiss Spotify as just another tech company, but to do so would be to ignore the way it has woven itself into our everyday existence. It has given sound to silence, comfort to solitude, and rhythm to the ordinary. It reminds us that no matter where we are, we are never truly alone because there is always a song waiting to be played, waiting to remind us that someone, somewhere, has felt exactly what we are feeling right now.

CHAPTER NINE

THE HAPPY SHOE

How do you build a company that people love? Not just a company that they buy from, but one they feel connected to, one they trust, one that makes them smile? Zappos found the answer, and it wasn't through advertising, aggressive sales, or clever marketing tricks. It was something simpler. Something rarer. It was kindness.

Zappos is not just about selling shoes. It is about selling happiness. At its core, this company understands something that most corporations forget, that customers are not just numbers, they are people. Real, messy, complicated, emotional people. And when you treat them as such, something incredible happens, they come back. Not because they have to, but because they want to.

The stories of Zappos' legendary customer service feel almost mythical. There are tales of representatives spending hours on the phone with customers, not to make a sale, but simply to listen and connect. There are stories of surprise upgrades, free returns with no questions asked, and employees who go to extraordinary lengths to make someone's day just a little bit better. These are not marketing gimmicks. They are the foundation of a company that understands that the way you make people feel is just as important as what you sell.

Zappos built a culture that valued joy over efficiency, human connection over rigid policies. And in doing so, it created something revolutionary, a business model that proved kindness is not just good ethics, but good business.

We live in a time where most customer service feels like a fight, where companies treat consumers as problems to be solved rather than people to be helped. But Zappos remains a beacon of what is possible when a business chooses empathy over profit. It is a reminder that, at the end of the day, we do not just buy products. We buy experiences. We buy trust. And we buy from the people who make us feel seen, heard, and valued.

CHAPTER TEN

REVOLUTION IN EVERY AISLE

For decades, grocery stores were just that, places to buy food, nothing more. They were sterile, impersonal, uninspiring. Then Whole Foods Market arrived, and suddenly, food shopping became something more. It became a statement. A movement. A rebellion against the artificial, the processed, the soulless.

Whole Foods did not just sell organic food, it sold a philosophy. It made people question what they were putting into their bodies. It made them think about where their food came from, who grew it, how it was made. It made eating real, unprocessed, ethically sourced food not just a privilege, but a priority.

But beyond the carefully curated shelves and eco-friendly initiatives, Whole Foods did something even more profound, it built a community. It made grocery shopping feel like an experience, a gathering place, a celebration of food as something more than just sustenance. It brought farmers and consumers together. It championed local businesses. It proved that ethical choices and financial success do not have to be mutually exclusive.

Whole Foods is not perfect. No company is. But what makes it special is its commitment to something bigger than profit. It fights for sustainability in an industry that often prioritizes convenience over conscience. It pushes for transparency in a market full of misleading labels. It has changed the way people think about food, and that is no small feat.

In a world where fast and cheap so often win, Whole Foods reminds us that food is more than just fuel. It is culture. It is connection. It is an opportunity to make choices that matter, not just for ourselves, but for the planet and the people who grow our food. And that is a legacy worth celebrating.

The Legacy Of Innovation

Business is often reduced to numbers. Profit margins, revenue growth, quarterly reports. But when you peel back the layers, when you strip away the corporate jargon and the balance sheets, what remains is something profoundly human. Behind every great company is not just a strategy but a story. A purpose. A desire to change the world in ways big and small.

Writing this book, I didn't just study businesses. I studied people. People who dared to think differently, who saw gaps in the world and had the courage to fill them. Yvon Chouinard, who built Patagonia not just to sell jackets but to save the planet. Elon Musk, who looked beyond the sky and saw a future among the stars. The founders of Warby Parker, who questioned why glasses, a necessity not a luxury, were priced out of reach for so many. Blake Mycoskie, who turned a simple shoe into a vehicle for change with TOMS. Ben Cohen and Jerry Greenfield, who proved that ice cream and activism could share the same cone. Tony Hsieh, whose vision for Zappos was never about selling shoes but about delivering happiness. The artisans of Etsy, who remind us that creativity still has value in a world of mass production. The engineers behind Spotify, who gave us the gift of endless music at our fingertips. The team at Whole Foods, who challenged an industry to think beyond cheap and convenient and instead to think about sustainability and health. And the pioneers of Beyond Meat, who took on the impossible challenge of making plant-based food mainstream.

What unites these businesses isn't just their success. It's their willingness to stand for something more. To be bold. To be different. To take risks in pursuit of a vision bigger than themselves. They remind us that a company can be more than a machine for making money, it can be a force for good. It can shift cultures, inspire generations, and rewrite the rules of what business is supposed to be.

I set out to write this book because I believe business is more than transactions and trends. I believe it is one of the most powerful tools we have to shape the world. And I believe that if we want to leave behind something meaningful, we must look beyond the bottom line. These companies have left a legacy, not just in their industries but in the way they have shaped the way we live, work, and think.

Maybe you are a dreamer, sitting on an idea that the world has told you is too unconventional, too ambitious, too different. Maybe you are an entrepreneur, wondering whether it's possible to build something that is both profitable and purposeful. Or maybe you are simply someone who wants to live in a world where businesses care about more than just their shareholders. If this book has shown you anything, I hope it is this. The businesses that change the world are not the ones that follow the rules. They are the ones that write their own.

So, the question is, what will you build? What legacy will you leave? The world does not need another ordinary company. It needs people willing to take a stand, to challenge the status quo, to believe that business can be a force for something greater. And if you are one of those people, then perhaps, one day, someone will be writing about the impact you left behind.

Because legacy is not about what we take. It is about what we give.

www.ingramcontent.com/pod-product-compliance
Lightning Source LLC
LaVergne TN
LVHW021202160826
845679LV00024B/2221

* 9 7 9 8 8 9 7 4 4 3 2 6 0 *